THE WISDOM

of the

PAGAN
PHILOSOPHERS

TIMOTHY FREKE
AND PETER GANDY

ℨ

First published in 1998 by Journey Editions, an imprint of
Periplus Editions (HK) Ltd., with editorial offices at
153 Milk Street, Boston, Massachusetts 02109.

Distributed by:
USA
Charles E. Tuttle Co., Inc. RR 1 Box 231-5
North Clarendon, VT 05759
Tel.: (802) 773-8930 Fax.: (802) 773-6993

Japan
Tuttle Shokai Ltd. 1-21-13, Seki
Tama-ku, Kawasaki-shi
Kanagawa-ken 214
Japan
Tel.: (044) 833-0225 Fax.: (044) 822-0413

Southeast Asia
Berkeley Books Pte. Ltd. 5 Little Road #08-01
Singapore 536983
Tel.: (65) 280-3320 Fax.: (65) 280-6290

ISBN 1-885203-54-3
The Catalog Card Number is on file with
the Library of Congress

Printed in Hong Kong

CONTENTS

Introduction

We have inherited a Victorian view of the ancient pagan philosophers as rather dry intellectuals, whose teachings are outdated and of interest only to Classic historians. Actually they were charismatic sages and wandering godmen, comparable to Hindu gurus, who taught the perennial spiritual philosophy. Pythagoras, for example, is remembered as a mathematician, yet he was also a mystic. He dressed in flowing white robes and wore a golden coronet on his head, he knew all of his own past lives and those of his followers, claimed to be able to hear the harmony of the universe which he called "the music of the spheres," was believed to have performed many miracles including reviving the dead, and was proclaimed a "god" by the thousands of devotees who surrounded him. Pythagoras was one of the first Greeks to visit Egypt where he spent twenty years being initiated into its ancient spirituality. He was the first man to call himself a philosopher and was an inspiration to all the great philosophers who came after him.

Paganism honors many gods, but like all polytheistic religions it also acknowledges a supreme transcendental One

God. This is the God of the philosophers. The other "gods" were regarded as powers and manifestations of this one ultimate divinity. The philosophers often ridiculed the absurd stories told of the gods as superstition. This led to them being persecuted as atheists and, as was the case for Socrates, being put to death. They were not concerned with the outer forms of religion, but with directly experiencing the mystical truth for themselves. Above the sanctuary at the Oracle of Delphi were inscribed the words "Know Your Self." This is the essence of Paganism. The philosophers taught that only through self-knowledge can we come to knowledge of the Oneness of God.

I. The One

The Pagan philosophers taught that everything is part of an interconnected whole. All things are subsumed within a supreme Oneness, that is God. God is the mind of the universe and his creation is his body. God is "Apollo" meaning "Not-Many" and also "Pan" meaning "All." The Oneness is divided by the strife between opposites so that it appears as many things. It is united by the healing power of love that embraces and transcends all opposition. Separate things are illusionary appearances. The Oneness of God is the underlying reality.

> **"** If you see things as they are here and now,
> you have seen everything
> that has happened from all eternity.
> All things are an interrelated Oneness. **"**

MARCUS AURELIUS

> " The infinite has no beginning. It is the beginning
> of all other things. It is divine,
> immortal, and indestructible. "

ANAXIMANDER

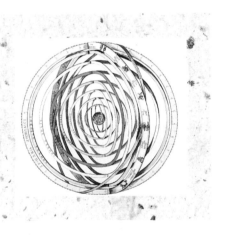

> " On one side is God,
> the active principle, who acts.
> On the other side is matter,
> the passive principle, that undergoes. "

PYTHAGORAS

66 Night and day,
winter and summer,
war and peace,
hunger and plenty,
these are all aspects of one God.
A fire takes on the aroma
of whatever spice is thrown in it. 99

HERACLITUS

66 There are two sides to this tale. On the one hand the
many unite to become the Oneness, and on the other
hand the Oneness divides to become the many.
Things continually shift between being united
by love and divided by strife. 99

EMPEDOCLES

How can all things be One,
yet each thing separate?

ORACLE OF ORPHEUS

We must begin by discriminating
between that which is and never
becomes, and that which is always
becoming and which never is.

PLATO

The sum of all that is has a soul.
God is the mind of the universe.

THALES

The One is God.

XENOPHANES

He is sacred, ineffable mind,
darting over the whole world
with his swift thoughts.

EMPEDOCLES

" Every thing contains a portion of all things,
but Consciousness is infinite, free, alone,
and mixed with nothing else.
Consciousness is pure and sublime.
It has knowledge of everything.
It controls all life, great and small.
It governs the spinning wheel of separateness
that divides things off one from the other.
It knows all that is, and things that are not,
and things that have been,
and things that shall be.
Consciousness arranges all things as they are,
including the rotating stars,
the sun, the moon, the air, and the ether. "

ANAXAGORAS

Why will you not admit that the universe is a conscious intelligence since conscious intelligences are born from it?

CICERO

66 God is the unity of Oneness
in which I dwelt myself
before I was snatched away
by the conflict of opposites
and born into the world of plurality
organized by strife. 99

EMPEDOCLES

*Appearances are a glimpse
of what is hidden.*

ANAXAGORAS

      ❝ He is too great
to be called by the name "God."
He is hidden,
yet obvious everywhere.
He is bodiless,
yet embodied in everything.
There is nothing that he is not.
He has no name,
because all names are his name.
He is the unity in all things,
so we must know him by all names
and call everything "God." **❞**

HERMES TRISMEGISTUS

There is one God, always
still and at rest,
who moves all things with
the thoughts of his mind.

XENOPHANES

The One is willing and reluctant
to be called "God."

HERACLITUS

The One is all things.
All things are One.

HERACLITUS

The universe is a single whole,
comprised of many parts
that are also wholes.

PLATO

II. Lovers of Wisdom

"**P**hilosopher" means "lover of Sophia the goddess of wisdom." The philosophers were not just great intellectuals, they were also devotees who treated truth as their beloved. Although they were accomplished scientists who knew the world was a sphere orbiting the sun hundreds of years before Kepler, they were also saintly mystics who reached beyond the intellect to direct intuitive knowledge of God. Ultimately, philosophy is about transcending all ideas and concepts and experiencing "Gnosis" – mystical enlightenment.

> The words of the philosophers promise us peace.
> If you will listen to me,
> whoever you are and whatever you do,
> you shall not grieve, you will not be angry,
> you will not be forced or blocked,
> but you will live without anxiety and suffering.
> Caesar did not and could not proclaim this peace,
> for it comes only from God.

EPICTETUS

Human opinions
are toys for children.

HERACLITUS

The wise exchange all
things for One thing;
but most people are like
full-fed cattle.

HERACLITUS

> **"** Life is a battlefield.
> You are a stranger sojourning in a foreign land.
> After fame comes oblivion.
> What is there that can support a human being?
> One thing only – philosophy. **"**

MARCUS AURELIUS

> **"** Because the One transcends all descriptions,
> you can form no conception of it,
> yet it is always present
> to those with strength to touch it. **"**

PLOTINUS

Pure philosophy is spiritual striving,
through constant contemplation,
to attain True Knowledge of the One-God.

HERMES TRISMEGISTUS

*No human being will ever
know the Truth, for even if
they happened to say it by chance,
they would not know they had done so.*

XENOPHANES

> *Discovering the Father and Creator of the universe is a supremely difficult task; and having found Him it would be impossible to tell anyone about Him.*
>
> PLATO

Diagoras was on a voyage when the sea became very rough. The nervous crew began muttering that it was because they were carrying on board someone who ridiculed the gods and religious superstition. Pointing out other ships also caught up in the same storm, Diagoras commented, "How remarkable! If you are right, every one of these vessels must also be carrying a Diagoras as a passenger."

Diagoras was admiring with a friend the many expensive votive monuments to the gods surrounding a temple in Samothrace. His friend explained to him that these structures had been erected in gratitude by those who, while in peril on the sea, had promised to honor the gods if divine intervention rescued them from a watery grave. The monuments were testimony to the efficacy of prayer and the power of the gods. Diagoras replied sardonically, "Just think how many more there would have been if all those who had drowned had also been able to set one up."

Human beings think of the gods as having been born, wearing clothes, speaking, and having bodies like their own. Ethiopians say the gods are black with snub-noses. Thracians say they have blue eyes and red hair. If cows and horses had hands they would draw pictures of the gods looking like cows and horses!

XENOPHANES

Much to his surprise, the Oracle of Delphi proclaimed Socrates to be the wisest man alive because he knew that he knew nothing.

" Is it possible to live abundantly with nothing,
no home, a beggar without a country? Look,
God has sent you someone to show you by his
example that it is possible. I have no home,
country, wife, or children, but only earth and
heaven and a simple blanket. But I am happy.
I am not anxious. I am free.

Look friends, how I have nothing and need
nothing. See, I am a homeless, landless exile;
and yet I live more free from troubles than
all the rich and powerful. "

EPICTETUS

28

To simply love God in thought
with singleness of heart,
and to follow the Goodness of his will
– this is philosophy,
unsullied by intrusive cravings
for pointless opinions.

HERMES TRISMEGISTUS

Life is like a cattle market.
Most people come to buy and sell; but
possessions and land, servants and social
standing, are all just worthless fodder.
Few come to the market simply for love
of the spectacle; wondering at what the
world is and who created it. Such
observers are ridiculed by the traders;
but then, if cows could speak they would
mock all those who cared about
anything but grass.

EPICTETUS

" What use are feet to a being that does not walk, or hands to a being that does not handle? We are inferior to the divine in every way, so why should we be similar to it in bodily shape? It is human virtue, not human form, that comes closest to the divine. If you ask me what is the nature and character of a divine being, I shall reply like Simonides who was asked this question by the tyrant Hiero. Simonides begged for a day's grace to consider the question, and then two days more, and then four days, and so on until Hiero became curious and asked why he kept begging for more time. Simonides replied, "Because the longer I contemplate the question, the more I am unable to answer it." **"**

COTTA THE STOIC

When the rulers of the city asked Anaxagoras what privileges they could honor him with after his death, he replied that children should be given a holiday each year on the anniversary of his passing.

Momus: "Zeus, I'm ashamed to mention all the ibises, monkeys, billy-goats and other beasts that have somehow been smuggled into Heaven. How can you bear to see them worshipped as gods? And you yourself, Zeus, how can you put up with those ridiculous ram's horns they stick on your head?"

Zeus: "You are right, Momus, these things are unseemly. Yet most of them are a matter of symbolism and someone who is not an initiate into the Mysteries really should not laugh at them."

LUCIAN

When Diogenes died at the age of 96 he asked
for his body to be carelessly thrown in a ditch
and sprinkled with dust. In fact his devoted
admirers buried him with full honors.

*Human beings entering life are like
those going to a public spectacle. Some
desire wealth and comfort. Some want
power and control. Some are ambitious
for glory. Those with purity and
integrity devote themselves to contemplation of the most beautiful things.
These may genuinely be called
"philosophers."*

PYTHAGORAS

Diogenes owned nothing and lived in a funerary pot outside the temple of Athene in Athens. He was once visited by Alexander the Great, who was so in awe of him that he offered to grant the great philosopher any request. Diogenes replied, "Please move yourself, you are blocking the sunlight." Alexander remarked, "If I were not Alexander, I would wish to be Diogenes."

> *Heraclitus was asked by the citizens of Ephesus to become a law-maker. He refused, replying, "If I did so, who would play with the children in the temple?"*

66 It is not bad luck, but right and just that you have found yourselves traveling this road, far from the beaten track followed by others. It is right that you should learn all things and develop the unshakable heart of well-rounded truth, unlike the opinions of men that contain no truth at all. You shall learn how mere appearances seem as though they actually exist. 99

PARMENIDES

III. Know Your Self

The Self is a part of God and our means of knowing God. This Self is not the "personality" – a word that comes from the Greek word "persona" meaning mask. It is the Higher Self or "Genius" that lies behind the mask of the illusionary ego-self. The Genius appears to us as a spiritual guide. It is our "conscience," meaning "with knowledge." The Pagan sages recognized this wise inner teacher as their true identity and so saw themselves as immortal gods, not transitory bodies and personalities. More than this, they discovered that the Genius is the one Consciousness that lives through all beings – the soul of the universe.

66 God has placed the Genius by the side of every human being to guide and protect them. The Genius doesn't sleep and cannot be deceived. Just as soldiers take an oath to honor no man above Caesar, it is right that you take an oath before the Genius, to honor yourself above all. 99

EPICTETUS

You have often heard me talk of a divine oracle or guide that comes to me. It is a kind of voice, that I first heard as a child. It always tells me what not to do, but never commands me to do anything. It is this voice that has, quite rightly I feel, deterred me from becoming a politician.

SOCRATES

> ❝ God is self originating and motherless,
> untaught and unshakeable;
> unnameable and possessing all names.
> We are parts of God, his angels.
> This then is the oracle's reply
> to the question concerning God's nature.
> He is all-seeing Consciousness.
> Pray to him at dawn, looking to the East. ❞

GREEK ORACLE

*Human beings were created to
contemplate and reflect the universe.
They are not themselves this great
perfection, but are particles of perfection.*

CICERO

*The warmth of life in every
human being is immortal.
It sees, hears, and knows all that
is and all that will be.*

HIPPOCRATES

*Man as he now is has
ceased to be the All.
But when he ceases to be
a separate individual,
he raises himself again
and permeates the universe.*

PLOTINUS

37

66 Few know how to help themselves
when they are beset by misfortune.
Bound by fate,
humanity runs an endless circle of sorrow.
Their grim companion
is disunity from themselves.

Father Zeus, free them from these great sufferings
and show every one of them
the Genius who is their guide. 99

PYTHAGORAS

I went in search of myself.

HERACLITUS

---

66 Who lives with the gods? Those who are always satisfied
with what has been assigned for them and who obey the
promptings of their Genius; a portion of Himself that
God has given to every human being to be their guide
and guardian, their intelligence and understanding. 99

MARCUS AURELIUS

Know Your Self

INSCRIPTION AT THE
ORACLE OF DELPHI

> 66 We should think of the most authoritative part
> of the soul as a guardian spirit given by God
> that lifts us to our heavenly home. 99

PLATO

> 66 You are a fragment torn from God.
> You have a portion of Him within you. 99

EPICTETUS

Although there is one Consciousness
that is common to all,
people act as if they had a
consciousness of their own.

HERACLITUS

The soul is a small portion of God.

DIOGENES

You are a soul carrying about a corpse.

EPICTETUS

Even if you travel everywhere
you will not find the limits of the soul,
so great is its nature.

HERACLITUS

*Just as children seem foolish
to adults, so humans seem foolish
to the gods.*

HERACLITUS

IV. Ethics

The Pagan philosophers teach that by cultivating goodness we can purify ourselves of our selfishness. This breaks the chains that bind us to our illusionary ego-self, freeing us to experience our true divine nature. Central to the Pagan path is accepting whatever life brings us as our divinely decreed fate; surrendering the illusion of personal power and recognizing ourselves as "puppets of God." This is not passive resignation, but actively engaging with things as they are by being a willing vehicle of God's unfolding purpose in the universe.

> *What is purity?*
> *Thinking only holy thoughts.*
>
> MOTTO OF THE HEALING
> SANCTUARY OF ASCLEPIUS

Although we cannot choose what happens to us, we can choose how we respond.

EPICTETUS

How lamentable it is that men blame the gods for their troubles, when their own wickedness brings them suffering over and above that which Destiny decrees for them.

ZEUS IN THE ODYSSEY

The beginning of philosophy is to become conscious of your own inadequacies and weaknesses.

Do you want to be good? Then first understand that you are bad.

EPICTETUS

44

“ We always revolve about the One,

but we do not always pay attention to it.

Like a chorus singing harmoniously around its conductor

becomes discordant when it turns away from him,

but sings beautifully when turned inward and fully attentive –

we similarly revolve around the Oneness of God,

but do not always look to him.

Yet when we do, we find our home and resting place.

Around him we dance the true dance;

God-inspired and no longer dissonant. ”

PLOTINUS

Common people retreat from the world
to country houses, the seashore or the
mountains, but it is always in your power
to retreat into yourself. Give yourself to
this retreat; renew and cleanse your
soul completely.

MARCUS AURELIUS

66 Someone who has used his life for learning true wisdom
and exercised his higher nature, if he finds the Truth,
is bound to have good thoughts and cannot fail to attain
immortality as completely as human nature allows. Because
he has always nurtured his divine essence in himself,
his guardian Genius, he is the happiest of people. 99

PLATO

*Extinguish violence more quickly
than you would a fire.*

*It is hard to fight the power of the passions,
but the price of failure is your soul.*

HERACLITUS

66 Happiness comes from understanding one basic principle.
Some things are within our control and some things are not.
Our opinions, ambitions, desires, and aversions are in our
control. We can change the contents of our inner character.
Our body, wealth, fame, and social status are not in our
control. They are external to us and not our concern. 99

EPICTETUS

" An unjust act always dishonors the perpetrator. We must cause no injury. Neither must we return injury for injury, as many people believe is right. We must injure no one at all. We must not retaliate or return evil for evil, whatever the evil we may have suffered ourselves. **"**

SOCRATES

Look closely. Know yourself. Question your genius. Do nothing without God, whether He teaches you by making you great or greatly plaguing you. This is the philosopher's way; to be flogged like an ass and to love those who beat him, to be the father and brother of all humanity.

EPICTETUS

" Do not afflict others with anything that you yourself would not wish to suffer. If you would not like to be a slave, make sure no one is your slave. If you have slaves, you yourself are the greatest slave, for just as freedom is incompatible with slavery, so goodness is incompatible with hypocrisy. **"**

EPICTETUS

Be like a steady promontory
against which continually
break the waves of life.

MARCUS AURELIUS

If someone speaks badly of you,
do not defend yourself against the
accusations, but reply: "You obviously
don't know about all my other vices,
otherwise you would have mentioned
these as well."

EPICTETUS

Accept all that happens, even that
which is unpleasant, because everything
is a part of the health of the universe
and the wealth of God.

MARCUS AURELIUS

*The Stoics believe that a wise man
is a friend of all other wise men, whether
educated or uneducated. There is nothing
more lovable than goodness and we should
love all those throughout the world who
have sought and found goodness.*

COTTA THE STOIC

66 O Universe!
Everything that is in harmony with you
is in harmony with me.

O Nature!
Nothing is too late or too early for me.
that is appropriate for you.

Everything is the fruit
that your seasons bring 99

MARCUS AURELIUS

*Human nature has
no better helper than love.*

SOCRATES

66 Do not pray for anything in particular for yourselves.
How do you know what is good for you? 99

PYTHAGORAS

66 Don't live by your own rules,
but in harmony with Nature. 99

EPICTETUS

51

Everything that happens is
just and fair to the gods,
but humans regard some things
as just and others as unjust.

HERACLITUS

A man's character is his fate.

HERACLITUS

All punishment is like therapy
for a soul that has gone wrong.

ALBINUS

Small-minded people blame others.
Average people blame themselves.
The wise see all blame as foolishness.

EPICTETUS

To get everything you want
is not a good thing.
Disease makes health seem sweet.
Hunger leads to the appreciation
of being full-fed.
Tiredness creates the enjoyment
of resting.

HERACLITUS

v. Death and Reincarnation

The philosophers teach that by "dying" as a separate ego-self, we can bring to life the Genius within us. This was the purpose of initiations in the pagan mystery religions. To be reborn in spirit the initiate underwent a ritual death. Apuleius describes himself as undergoing a "voluntary death." If we do not awaken spiritually while alive, then physical death will only lead to further rebirths in an endless cycle of reincarnation that Pythagoras called "The Grievous Wheel." However, when we spiritually awaken we will realize that ultimately there is only the One Consciousness of God, the supreme soul or Genius, that is transmigrating through all forms.

> " Life would be a feast to the wicked
> and death a godsend, were it not for
> the immortality of the soul. "
>
> PYTHAGORAS

> 66 The highest of our initiations in this world is only
> a dream of the true vision and initiation of death.
> The Mysteries have been carefully conceived to awaken
> memories of the sublime things to come. 99

PLUTARCH

> 66 Having been born again and again,
> the soul sees everything that exists
> and has knowledge of all. 99

SOCRATES

66 Earthly death liberates Consciousness and
the soul from the body. The soul flies up to a space
between the Earth and Moon where it is punished
and purified. The purified souls of the just enjoy the
delights of paradise on the Moon. If they avoid sin
they are not punished with reincarnation,
and the second death occurs that liberates
Consciousness to return to the sun, its source. 99

PLUTARCH

The best life is spent preparing for death.

PLATO

---

66 It is our fear of death that terrifies us.
You can think about a thing
in many ways.
Scrutinize your idea of death.
Is it true? Is it helpful?
Don't dread death or suffering.
Dread your fear of death
and suffering. 99

EPICTETUS

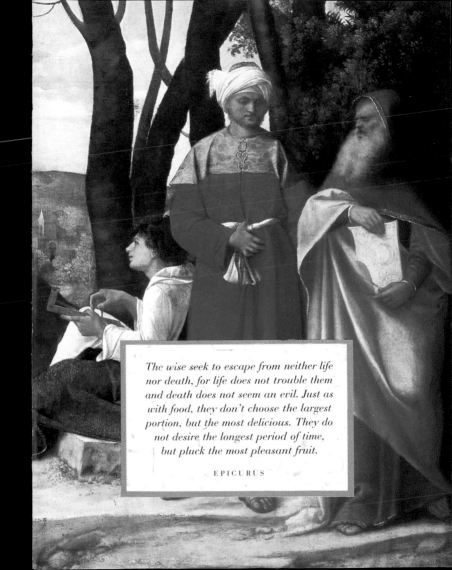

The wise seek to escape from neither life nor death, for life does not trouble them and death does not seem an evil. Just as with food, they don't choose the largest portion, but the most delicious. They do not desire the longest period of time, but pluck the most pleasant fruit.

EPICURUS

66 Birth is not the beginning of life –
only of an individual awareness.
Change into another state is not death –
only the ending of this awareness.
Most people are ignorant of the Truth,
and therefore afraid of death,
believing it to be the greatest of all evils.
But death is only the dissolution
of a worn out body.
Our term of service as guardians of the world
is ended when we are freed
from the bonds of this mortal frame
and restored,
cleansed, and purified,
to the primal condition of our higher nature. 99

HERMES TRISMEGISTUS

*Nothing comes into existence and nothing
passes away. Everything is compounded
from and dissolves into That Which Is.
Coming into being is just composition, and
perishing is simply dissolution.*

ANAXAGORAS

When we live our souls are dead,
but when we die our souls
revive and live again.

HERACLITUS

The soul is immortal. After death it
transmigrates into other beings. All sentient
beings are part of one great family.

PYTHAGORAS

At the moment of death the soul must be
as it is during the Mysteries: free from
any blemish, passion, envy, or anger.

PORPHYRY

There has been a time
when I was a young man,
and a young girl,
and a bush, a bird,
a scaly fish gleaming in the ocean.

EMPEDOCLES

Perhaps death is life
and in the other world
life is thought of as death.
Who knows?

EURIPIDES

The publishers would like to thank the following for the use of pictures:

Bridgeman Art Library: pp. 4, 9, 13, 16, 18, 24, 26, 31, 35, 36, 39, 42, 46, 55, 57

e.t. archive: pp. 40, 59

Vanessa Fletcher: p. 11

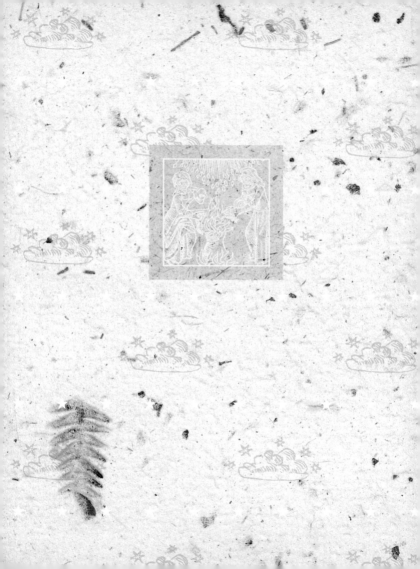